The Om
CONTEMPLATIONS

The Om
CONTEMPLATIONS

BRENDAN LLOYD

Copyright © 2017 Brendan Lloyd

ISBN: 978-1-925681-15-4
Published by Vivid Publishing
A division of Fontaine Publishing Group
P.O. Box 948, Fremantle
Western Australia 6959
www.vividpublishing.com.au

Cataloguing-in-Publication data is available from the National Library of Australia

Contents

Introduction

This book contains 'spiritual poetry' written while I was undergoing a mini 'Manic Experience' in Mid-August 2017 ('Manic Experiences' are described in detail in my previous non-fiction book *Out Of This World*). While my experiences in August 2017 definitely qualify as a 'Manic Experience', it was maybe a tenth of the intensity of previous experiences, and I may write about it later – either a revised and expanded version of 'Out Of This World', or in some other format.

While in an elevated state (or 'altered state' if you prefer), I was mentally chanting the Hindu 'Om Tat Sat' and 'Sat Chit Ananda' to calm myself mentally, and began writing by hand a type of 'Om-inspired poetry'. The quality of my handwriting is generally quite embarrassing, but sometimes the old fashioned 'pen & paper' gets the job done – obviously people who invented Pen & Paper RPGs must have thought so! Not that I've played any Pen & Paper RPGs, but pen & paper (and sometimes pencil & paper) are good for jotting down on the spot, and computers with their fancy-pants word processing are for 'fine-tuning' and making things look more 'professional'. You never know when keeping a pen and plenty of blank paper handy will come in handy – the old-fashioned 'jotting down' is a time-honoured tradition! That, or 'Pen & Paper RPG' should be renamed 'Computer & Micro-soft Word RPG', but somehow I don't think the name will stick.

Speaking of names, it's a pity it's 'contemplations' and not 'com-templations' – you *can* get 'om' from contemplations if you look hard enough, but 'contemplations' sounds more profound than 'The Om Meditations' – you've probably heard 'contemplation' at least a few times, but how many times have you heard con-templation*s*? There are people who have contemplated and do 'contemplate' other, unsavoury things that definitely are *not* a sign of good mental health, so why not contemplate something that *improves* mental health instead of *imploding* mental health?

The poetry contained in this book was written over the span of about a week and was mostly unedited in the process of compil-ing for this book. While in the elevated state I mentioned, I drew from many sources when writing the 'Contemplations' – the Bible, Hip-Hop slang, U.S 'Deep South' accents, the inspiration was coming to me, and I was giving it form (and no, I didn't have Patrick Swayze's ghostly hands guiding mine – because that would just be plain weird, wouldn't it?).

I also used older versions of English (e.g Shakespearean) where it felt natural – sometimes older versions of English have a certain 'flavour' that's difficult or sometimes impossible to replicate in Modern English. Besides, I'm sure some modern writers fanta-sise about being able to be as much of a wordsmith as Shake-speare (and hopefully don't fantasise about being an 'Agent' named Smith). We don't really need 'blacksmiths' these days, but we can always use more *word*smiths. I mean, think about it – *Word*press and Microsoft *Word* – some enterprising people must have really 'dug' a certain Bible passage about 'the Word'. Word of advice: don't mention 'bird' anywhere in vicinity of 'the Word' (Family Guy reference for those who don't know).

The topic of 'words' could easily be (and for all I know, already is) the subject of an entire book or even series of books – what if Jesus' "I came not to bring peace, but to bring a sword" (Matthew 10:34) had been "I came not to bring peace, but to bring a *word*"? How many expressions and phrases have "word" in them? E.g "A word to the wise", "a word of advice", "a quick word". Even that topic is something that could be contemplated over endlessly, but if you can't stand long-winded speeches, books, etc, luckily, this book won't be doing that (at least not 'endlessly', anyway).

I designed this book to be succinct and compact – meaning it squeezes a lot into a tiny package (which if you ordered the paperback version of this book, is exactly what you received in the mail). "I love massive, phonebook-thickness tomes that can't fit into my backpack", said almost no one ever - even nerds probably just get the eBook version instead. At least, the ones who *aren't* already busy designing the next Apple product.

I find writing, both fiction and non-fiction to be quite cathartic, and if you don't identify as a 'Creative', that's fine – speaking from my own experience, 'Creatives' have a different perspective than the majority of non-creatives and their brain is wired differently (you don't need science to fact-check that, do you? Just checking).

As a creative, many of us would be perceived as 'daydreaming' a lot, and to an extent, we are. Creative inspiration can come at any time, in any place, or anything or anyone, and we have to always be ready when inspiration comes – most non-creatives I've seen are very linear-minded and can work a very repetitive sets of tasks in a job every day - from the perspective of a Creative - almost 'robotically' without ever really being distracted by flights of imagination, flashes of inspiration and your brain feeling like a wall of security camera TV feed with something different happening on each screen. I read something online written by someone who is also a Creative, and they described feeling their mind was doing heaps of different things at once and their inability to hold down a regular, 9-5 job. When I read that, I thought 'Yep! I know *that* feeling!'. Feeling 'switched on' is great for creativity, not so great for living day-to-day.

Take a crack at non-fiction if creativity's not really your thing, I believe virtually everyone can benefit from writing non-fiction – otherwise we wouldn't have famous people who wrote an autobiography or memoirs. If they were already a celebrity, they're not exactly writing an autobiography because they don't think they're famous enough (well, *some* might), they're writing because they want other people to benefit from their experiences and insight (read "Out Of This World" and you'll see what I mean, if that's not too much of an egotistical thing to say. One's 'horn' probably gets broken one way or another if it gets used too often, either from overuse or 'unforeseen accident' [which, let's be honest, was really on purpose]).

I hope that the poetry in this book either inspires you to write your own poetry, or that a significant passage sticks with you that you reflect on over and over, continuing to gain new insight – that it guides you to 'contemplate' its meaning. If you want a book that 'contemplates' the 'meaning of life', you've bought the wrong book! Try Monty Python, maybe?

O-OMG!

If you read the introduction and somehow resisted the urge to skim ahead to the poetry, you'll remember I mentioned two Hindu mantras - 'Om Tat Sat', and 'Sat Chit Ananda'. First, let me give a general translation.

'Om Tat Sat' means "Om, that is Truth", "Om, it is Reality", "Om it is good". There's information available on Wikipedia and elsewhere on the internet, which may not seem much at first glance, but if you were to contemplate on the significance of 'Om Tat Sat', I have no doubts a guru could devote an entire book to it (one much thicker than any non-fiction book *I'll* ever write – or attempt to write - I think it's safe to say).

'Sat Chit Ananda' essentially translates as "existence, consciousness, and bliss", and there's quite a substantial amount of information about it.

I'm mostly familiar with these two mantras through reading the Bhagavad Gita, which, besides sounding awesome to say, is only one part of the fabulously rich Hindu tradition – the *good* (spiritual) kind of 'fabulously rich', not the egotistical one. The 'New

Age' cliché of women in a yoga pose chanting only the word 'Om' repeatedly is quite absurd – from my own experience, I've found only chanting 'Om' on its own has minimal effect which I've found to be virtually useless for rapid calming, and unless you're aiming to set or break the Guiness World Record for 'number of consecutive 'Om's chanted', use a more effective mantra.

By alternating mentally chanting these two mantras, I was able to 'get into a groove' mentally despite being 'elevated', not unlike the lyrics of The Beatles 'Across the Universe', and I was getting them down on paper as quickly as I could (there weren't any paper cups nearby being filled with endless rain, though). Before Manic Experience symptoms developed in August 2017, I essentially had not been chanting these two mantras at all, now I use them much more frequently – I wouldn't call them 'go-to' mantras, though.

While there's also the Buddhist mantra 'Om Mani Padme Hum' (which, as an English speaker, I find easier to pronounce 'Om Mani Padme Hom' [e.g due to English words like 'hominid' and 'hommus'], I haven't used it enough to vouch for its effectiveness for rapid calming – I mostly listen to song recording versions of it from time to time.

I *would* recommend though, that 'Om Mani Padme Hum' or 'Om Mani Padme Hom' (if you prefer my pronounciation) instead of just 'Om' repeatedly – let's be honest, the *yoga* is what those women are benefitting from, not their occasional utterance of a single 'Om' ('New Age Nonsense' at its finest!). Anyone notice they virtually always show women doing yoga and the only man is usually the yoga instructor? Do men only do yoga by watching a DVD and 'check out' the well-toned women? Come on, men, fess up!

My advice to anyone who dismisses the concept of mantras – try them first before you knock them, and keep trying them. My question to any skeptic or atheists thinking to 'outsmart' the concept of mantras by expecting amazing, immediate results, then claiming, 'oh, well, it didn't achieve what I expected it to straight away, therefore it doesn't work at all' - how many scientific discoveries of something 'invisible' like Infra-Red and magnetic fields were made by assuming they didn't exist, then making no effort to *prove* they exist?

If science can't already, soon they'll be able to scientifically measure the health benefits of mentally repeating mantras – if you're an atheist, are you *really* going to argue with the science?

Mantras aren't as foreign of a concept as you might think – businesses, organisations and corporations use a form of mantras all the time in marketing. A marketing slogan is essentially a type of mantra – and I'm sure you'll agree they're effective. In the West – slogan: scientifically verified, mantra: mystical pseudo-science. In the East: slogan: materialistic self-promotion, mantra: ancient wisdom.

Can someone please arrange for 'East' and 'West' to have a private meeting?

The Om Contemplations

Om, it is pure, it is a renewer

Om, delusion is confusion

Om, believe not every spirit, but test them, lest rise be given to false prophets

Om, let not the dominion of sorrow taint your thoughts for tomorrow

Om, what mere Man – or Woman – can call themselves 'the Highest Truth', surely a God 'up there' must curse their hubris, oh, surely He knew this

Om, God is love

Om, God is hope

Om, God is compassion

Om, God is Justice

Om, God is wisdom

Om, God is empathy

Om, God is gracious

Om, God is the Way, the Truth, the Power

Om, God is faith

Om, God is Mindful

Om, God is blissful

Om, 'God is God'

Om, God is the Alpha and Omega

Om, God is chaos

Om, God is freedom

Om, God is Agápē

Om, God is selfless

Om, God is beyond good and evil

Om, God is Hallowed

Om, God is the Known Unknown

Om, God is life

Om, God seeks, and He shall find

Om, God is one

Om, God is mercy

Om, God is sanctuary

Om, God is the Kingdom, God is in the heart

Om, God is the jailer

Om, God is the sacred yet profane

Om, God is The Name

Om, God is the fault

Om, God is the vault

Om, God is most, God is the least

Om, God is the humour, God is the rumour

Om, God be savin', ain't a haven for your misbehavin'

Om, God ain't craven, God ain't ravin'

Om, Hell's bells dispel bad spells

Om, knows best; Om, it tests; Om, it is success

Om, God is the judge, Om may begrudge

Om, God is time, yet no rhyme

Om, God is the gift and the gab

Om, God is a joke, yet the joker

Om, God helps those who can help themselves

Om, God is 'dope', phat will divine

Om, God is a wonder, yet a blunder, God will steal your thunder

Om, don't know jack, just send it back, don't attack the messengers

Om, hark herald angels sing, don't really need a damn thing, wing and a prayer, yet you care, yet you care

Om, elicit hope, however you cope

Om, that which you imitate, shall surely be your template, perhaps surely, this is fate

Om, a shining example let us not define, that which is your line, perhaps this too, is divine

Om, hatin' ain't makin' a penny or dime

Om, that which we know is good, that which is fine, that which is divine, lo, and behold, Thy Kingdom come. *God is the glory, the truth, the Kingdom, the heartful, the artful*

Om, delight in God, He who modifies – testify to His glory, His names be praised!

Om, to each his own, of whom shall we speak who is of lordly renown?

Om, Thy will create, oh, please let us alter fate

Om, behold, for God shall do anew, renew, review. The imagination, that, verily, shall we sing praises. Verily, must we deny the litanies of angels? Though one speak tongues of angels, in their heart, they know only the tongues of devils

Om, that is the death of the spirit, do not heed it, there are none who shall need it

Om, that which is truth,

Om, that which is wisdom,

Om, that which is impermanent,

Seek not its exterminant

Om, praise God for that which is God's, Om, praise beings for that which is being

Om, that which lords itself over, for naught but narcissism, shall surely fall below

Om, that which is both impure and corrupt, surely must know stigma

Om, curse that which aught know stigma, bless that which aught be taught, lest wisdom sink like a stone into the well of oblivion, befalling a mindless dominion

Om, dominion of mindlessness, hopelessness, foolishness, faithlessness, meaninglessness, wrathfulness, callousness; may God banish these evils from our sight, may God have mercy on this perversity

Om, shall we rejoice, for in diversity, that which is something unique, shall find its place in time and space, its rhyme, its season, its reason

Om, that which flies in the face of logic, must stand, then, perish the thought

Om, misnomer, is no joke, one-hit K.O, Game Over

Om, oh litany of lies, your disguise, for want of your deceit, your name dies

Om, oh, say can't you see, what you're aiming to be, why so proudly, why so loudly?

Om, be thee a seeker; if a writer, tweaker; be whatever thee be, be meek, of the spiritual, be ye worthy to peek

Om, vision, indecision, division, DIE-Vision, incision of revision, woe unimagination, it knows not its season, its purpose, its reason

Om, unimagination, unbecoming, unceasing, decreasing, releasing, unleash, undo, revise, speak truth, not lies

Om, dark dominion of opinion, seek not to be its minion

Om, two steps backwards, lack words, too absurd

Om, the pyramid is inverted, preaching to the converted, reverse the perverse, oh, that we curse

Om, curse only the perverse, it could be worse

Om, seek to invert the negative, seek not to pervert the positive

Om, be good and expect good, thoughts are like food,

*don't think what you can't swallow, don't think only
what is hollow*

*Om, what is, what shall be, these are the workings of
Infinity*

*Om, 'As Above, So Below'; Thy will be done on Earth
as it in Heaven, for what it is worth, God save this
Earth*

Suggested Mantras

The following are either mantras I personally have used, or have invented – by expanding the definition of 'mantra' somewhat to apply to any desired language, rather than simply its 'tradition-al' meaning of a Sanskrit phrase. I have been using mantras in three languages: Sanskrit, Hebrew and English, but if English is your second or third language, feel free to translate the English mantras into your native language if it feels more comfortable for you.

The mantras in this section are all ones that I've used myself and I can vouch for their effectiveness in achieving mental peace – Hebrew and English mantras are mostly ones that I've discov-ered myself by 'tinkering' [experimentation].

You can repeat them as many times as desired, but I would rec-ommend a minimum of three times per mantra.

You can chant aloud if no one else can hear or won't be bothered by your mantras, or you can chant mantras mentally (which has the added bonus of being able to be done anywhere you go because no one else can hear it). If you're feeling particular-ly stressed, have racing thoughts, or feeling out of sorts, then chant mentally wherever you happen to be at that moment, and continue chanting until you feel calmer, and you can choose to alternate between mantras for variety if you want to.

Don't expect immediate results with mantras – from my experience, it's like using exercise and training to improve your physical fitness: it takes time and effort, and you need to maintain your routine to have lasting benefits to your 'mental fitness' [if that's not already a legitimate phrase, it is *now*!].

Feel free to 'tinker' with other languages and see if you can discover even more mantras – the beauty of mantras is that many of the best ones haven't been discovered yet! Is there such a thing as a 'Mantra-ologist'? Who for once is *not* Hindu? There *should* be – just don't ask about career pathways!

Sanskrit Mantras:

Om Tat Sat

Sat Chit Ananda

(These two I explained in the introduction, and no further explanation is required)

Om Shanti, Shanti, Shanti Om

Hebrew Mantras:

"Hallel El Elyon" (Hebrew: "Praise God Most High") – I have found this one to be particularly effective for relaxation, particularly following it with the word "hallel" three times, in a pseudo 'Hare Krishna' manner. This mantra lends serious 'cred' to Hebrew being considered a sacred language – "el" appears three times consecutively in this mantra, and there seems to be a massive amount of energy in this mantra (considering the translation, if 'God' exists, there's your explanation). It's completely possible to 'give thanks to God' without this mantra, but this mantra seems to add an element of sacredness.

"Barukh Atah, [insert name]" (Hebrew: "You are blessed/Blessed are you, [insert name]") – this mantra is mainly for blessing a person, though if you have self-worth issues you could try using your own name.

"El lekadesh atah" (Modern Hebrew: "God sanctify you") – this mantra is best used in conjunction with the previous mantra, and can also be combined with the "Hallel El Elyon" mantra.

"Lerappei, Lesalek ra'al, leshakem, [insert name]" (Modern Hebrew: "Heal, Detoxify, Rehabilitate, [insert name]") – this mantra is for powerful healing, and again, lends serious 'cred' to Hebrew being a sacred language. Repeating it a few times has a mystical feeling to it.

English Mantras:

"Love is Creation" – I've had enormous success achieving mental peace with this particular mantra, an 'aura of peace' sometimes surrounds me after using this mantra and it's fairly easy to remember. A friend asked whether reversing the word order to

'Creation is Love' would be as effective, but personally I feel that there are some forms of 'creation' that are quite far removed from love (for example, creating nuclear weapons, or creating a totalitarian state), and that "(Unconditional) Love is (Unlimited) Creation" versus "(Every form of) Creation is Love" are not identical in meaning, and some forms of creation are not love at all. You could however use a mantra like "Love for All Creation" or "Love Creates" or even "Love Creates Unconditionally", but these two are not ones that I've used personally.

"Hallowed is El Elyon, Creator of All That Is" ("All That Is" is essentially equivalent to the religious term "All Creation") – this is also a very effective mantra, but because of its length, it's difficult to repeat continuously. I've found this mantra to be most useful if in an elevated or partially 'Manic' state, and is like 'bringing out the big guns'. Interestingly, some translations of 'Om Tat Sat' render it as 'All That Is'.

"Blessed be, blessed be, blessed be Infinity" – this mantra is derived from the Wiccan blessing "blessed be", a general statement of positive intent (as opposed to criminal intent which stands in the way of Law and Order) – I haven't used this one much, but feel free to substitute the word 'Infinity' for something more specific if you prefer.

"Love unto others" – Very Biblical-sounding ("Do unto others as you would have them do unto you" - Matthew 7:12), but that's probably the point - love in the sense of agápē.

"Faith in love" – this mantra is best used when you are dealing with feelings of there being too much hatred, violence and injustice in the world (if you've been disturbed by watching the news or reading the newspaper/reading news online), the Steve Winwood song 'Higher Love' comes to mind.

Recommended Further Reading:

Arbeau, Michelle. *The Energy of Words*. Llewellyn Publications, U.S, 2013

Hicks, Esther and Jerry. The Teachings of Abraham®. *Manifest Your Desires: 365 Ways to Make Your Dreams A Reality*. Hay House, 2008

https://en.wikipedia.org/wiki/Om_Tat_Sat

https://en.wikipedia.org/wiki/Satcitananda

OTHER BOOKS BY THIS AUTHOR

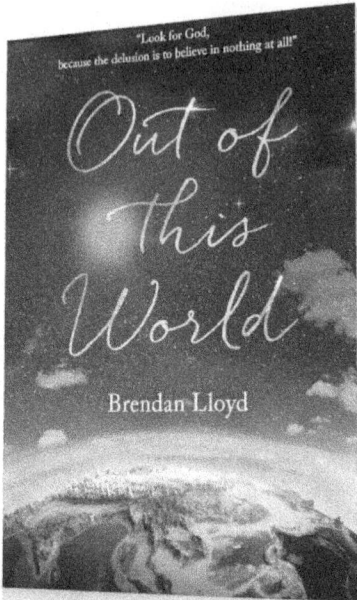

Out of This World
By Brendan Lloyd
Published by Vivid Publishing
ISBN: 978-1-925442-06-9

"Look for God, because the delusion is to believe in nothing at all!"

Have you ever considered spirituality but decided you couldn't make sense of all the jargon? You're not alone. Why settle for 'New Age' when you don't understand the Age-Old?

In this book, you'll discover real experiences and real insight – nothing fictional, or second-hand (except maybe this book one day). If you don't think (even slightly) differently after reading this book, either you're not thinking enough, or you didn't stop and think 'Why are we here?'

To quote the original Matrix film, 'Free your mind'; discover possibilities you thought were impossible, when you already knew the Mission was Impossible. But this one doesn't come with popcorn!

I'm not here to tell you to 'look within', or that 'the Kingdom of God is within', I'm here to tell you – look for God, because the delusion is to believe in nothing at all!

www.vividpublishing.com.au/outofthisworld